Praise for The Connector's Way

"In a world where people are looking for the 'one big thing' that will change their fortunes, this book rem... is rarely the answer. It is often a seri................................ difference. Best of all, the small thin............... are all doable."

                —Ric

"The single best book I've read on how to build lasting relationships. I found myself writing notes after every chapter and have referred back to the stories over and over. If you are in any kind of business or role where relationships or referrals are your lifeblood (and who's not?), do yourself a favor and read this book."

                —Michael Knouse, business and performance coach

"I'm so grateful for this book, since it inspired my successful business plan this year. Its simple yet powerful rules for building business one relationship at a time would work well for companies of any size and in any industry."

           —Tammy Wittren, loan originator, Guild Mortgage Company

"This book illustrates the best practices of great connectors in an easy-to-read, fun story. It is a reminder that good things happen naturally when we serve others."

           —Paul Witkay, founder and CEO, Alliance of Chief Executives

"Even in this digital age, business-to-business transactions (and specifically insurance) are about relationships. This book reignites the passion behind relationship building. I purchased 100 copies to pass out to my sales team."

  —Garth Hamilton, chief sales officer, HUB International Northwest

"If you're seeking to grow your client base, look no further. You'll learn the fundamentals of building successful, quality connections that enrich your life professionally and personally."

                —Randi Guthard, vice president & private client
                relationship manager, First Tennessee Bank

THE CONNECTOR'S WAY

Patrick Galvin

THE CONNECTOR'S WAY

**A STORY ABOUT BUILDING BUSINESS
ONE RELATIONSHIP AT A TIME**

PATRICK GALVIN

JRP

JOSEPH RUDOLPH PUBLISHERS • PORTLAND, OREGON

The Connector's Way:
A Story About Building Business One Relationship at a Time

Published by Joseph Rudolph Publishers,
www.josephrudolphpublishers.com

© 2016 Patrick Galvin. All rights reserved.

For discounts on bulk purchases or to hire
the author to speak to your organization,
please contact patrick@galvanizinggroup.com.

ISBN: 978-0-9828680-8-9 trade paperback
       978-0-9828680-9-6 electronic book

Editing: Kristi Hein
Book design and composition: Dick Margulis
Cover design: Ranilo Cabo

MANUFACTURED IN THE UNITED STATES OF AMERICA

Fourth printing

To my wife Ellen and daughter Anya, who keep me connected to everything that really matters.

Contents

As a professional speaker and relationship marketer, I've spoken with many people struggling to build business relationships that lead to loyalty, referrals, and sales. In this fictional story, Robert Hanson, whose insurance agency is on the brink of bankruptcy, meets two mentors and natural connectors who show him that the keys to success are simpler than he imagined.

In fact, the simplicity of building relationships is what inspired this book. We are inundated every day with marketing messages that tell us the path to building better business relationships lies with the newest technology and the latest social networking sites. The pitches are compelling—on multiple occasions, I've found myself eagerly awaiting a smartphone release or signing up for the flavor-of-the-moment social networking site that promises to make it easier than ever to build my network. My expectations are never met.

We can become so enamored with technology that we tune out the people around us. Need proof? Just look around the next time you're at a restaurant. You'll likely see couples and families silently staring at their screens instead of talking and enjoying each other's company.

At its very best, technology lets us build on our real-world relationships. All examples involving technology in *The Connector's Way* demonstrate how it can be used to strengthen rather than replace how we connect personally.

The motto at my company is "Nothing happens behind a desk." I need to be out in the world building relationships in order to grow our business. I adamantly believe that all business is personal. I agree wholeheartedly with Bob Burg, coauthor of *The Go-Giver*, who wrote: "All things being equal, people will do business with, and refer business to, those people they know, like, and trust."

I hope you enjoy reading this book as much as I enjoyed writing it. While the main character is an insurance agency owner, the lessons he learns apply to anybody looking for business success through better relationships.

Good luck building your business, one relationship at a time, and I hope to have the opportunity to connect with you in person someday!

Patrick Galvin

Introduction

I'M VERY SORRY, SIR, but your charge was declined," said the perky young woman working at the back of the crowded auditorium.

Robert Hanson felt his face flush and sweat trickle down his forehead as dozens of people anxiously jostled behind him.

He took back his business credit card and handed her his personal card. "Try this one."

She swiped it through the handheld reader—and smiled. "Perfect! It went through without a hitch. Enjoy your purchase and the rest of the event."

Later, as Robert walked the mile from the auditorium to his motel through cold driving rain, he wondered whether it had been a wise decision to spend $1,495 for three workbooks and a USB flash drive with training videos.

He had chosen to stay in a budget motel in a rundown part of town, since it offered much cheaper lodging than the four-star conference hotel where the Mega Business Builder Retreat was being held. Even minding his budget carefully, he had maxed out his business credit card on expenses for the two-day event:

registration fee, round-trip airfare halfway across the country, lodging, ground transportation, and meals.

While famous speakers had energized him during the conference for "business owners seeking mega growth," he still had no concrete plan for getting Hanson Insurance Agency, the ninety-three-year-old company that his great-grandfather had started, into the black. He desperately hoped that the kit he had just purchased would provide him with practical tactics that went beyond the inspirational *you-can-achieve-it-if-you-can-dream-it* messages that he had heard throughout the event.

As he sidestepped puddles, Robert felt sorry for himself. He was fifty years old, and he felt like his chance to succeed in life was slipping away. He remembered how optimistic he had been ten years ago, when he took over the family business after his father's death. At the time, the agency had a dozen loyal employees, with longtime clients fueling growth through their referrals to friends, relatives, and professional colleagues.

But over the past decade, competition had proved to be far more intense than Robert had anticipated. Large insurance carriers were spending billions of dollars on advertising campaigns to convince people to buy insurance directly from them rather than through small independent insurance agencies like his. Robert felt helpless as he watched policy renewals and referrals dry up.

Sitting in a rickety dining chair at a small desk, in a room that reeked of mold and cigarette smoke,

Robert looked through his briefcase for a stack of bills so he could see why his business credit card had been declined. He found the credit card bill and gulped at the balance: more than $50,000. It included a large cash advance that he had recently taken out to cover payroll expenses. He had no idea how he was going to pay that balance off. It had been more than six months since he had written a check for more than the minimum payment on any of his credit cards. If the agency's revenue didn't experience a dramatic turnaround, he might need to lay off employees or confront the stark reality of having to go out of business.

Robert had another reason for that sinking feeling in the pit of his stomach: his adjustable rate home mortgage loan payment had just jumped upward. The decision to buy a "dream home" ten years ago now seemed like a colossal mistake. He dreaded having to tell his wife, Marion, that they might need to sell the home that they both loved and move into a small apartment to keep the agency going.

Robert removed the USB flash drive from the Mega Business Builder Kit he had purchased and plugged it into his laptop computer. He launched the first video in a twenty-part series for business owners looking to achieve "mega growth." But after watching just five minutes, he slammed his laptop shut in disgust. Rather than specific recommendations, the video offered inspirational platitudes similar to those he had heard throughout the conference. The only specific ideas were pitches for website redesign, search engine optimization, and other expensive marketing services that he could ill afford.

Feeling the shooting pains of a stress-induced migraine headache, Robert lay down on the lumpy mattress, its coils digging into his spine. He closed his eyes, trying to come up with something positive to say to his wife and daughter when they asked him what he learned at the conference. But his concentration only increased the intensity of his headache.

1

Birthday

ROBERT WAS DEEP IN his worries as he walked into the lobby of Hillhaven Retirement Community. The brassy notes of big band music jolted him back to reality. As he made his way to the dining hall, he was surprised to hear his mother's distinctive laugh. He couldn't recall having heard her sound so happy since his father died.

Stepping into the dining hall, Robert was astounded to see his mother pushing a wheelchair around the glossy wood parquet dance floor. She spun the chair to face Robert, and his eyes locked on its occupant, a diminutive old man with a thick silver handlebar mustache that didn't obscure a wide grin.

"So you must be young Mr. Hanson, the insurance mogul. Your mother just can't stop bragging about you."

Robert reached out to shake the hand of Fred Cheevers. He quickly pulled back in embarrassment when he saw that Fred was missing his right arm.

"Gotcha!" Fred said with obvious glee. "I lost that one in World War II. No worries, though. I wouldn't know what I would do with it, anyway."

Robert laughed nervously. Fred flashed him a reassuring smile, showing off a set of pearly white dentures.

"Don't worry," Fred said. "I could never be upset with you after all the good you've done this old soldier. My life has been wonderful ever since you brought Joan here." Fred turned to wink at Robert's mother.

Robert looked at her too. His mother looked completely different from the lonely woman he had moved into the retirement community just three months ago. He looked around the dining hall and saw that the other residents were enjoying themselves, also. The festively decorated room was packed with seniors, chatting, singing, and dancing.

Robert noticed a man who looked to be in his seventies, in an elegant doubled-breasted grey pinstripe suit, walking to the podium at the front of the room. The man cleared his throat a couple of times before speaking into the microphone with a strong and confident tone.

"Thank you all for coming to my father, Fred Cheevers,' one hundredth birthday party. Years ago, he told me that he wanted to have a hundred people celebrate his centennial. Well, since there are more than two hundred of you here, we'll just have to make tonight's party last at least another hundred years." The room erupted in laughter.

The good spirits were hard for Robert to fathom. Some partygoers had oxygen tanks strapped to their wheelchairs. Most looked quite frail. He wondered how a group of people facing the challenges of old age could be so positive and energetic.

Later, he felt a tap on his shoulder: it was the man who had spoken at the podium. "Hey, this is a party, not a funeral. Or are you just feeling blue because you don't have beautiful grey hair like the rest of us?"

Robert felt awkward. He didn't normally wear his emotions on his sleeve. "It's kind of a long story," he said, avoiding the man's gaze.

"Well, I love long stories, but I won't press you for it in the midst of a birthday party," the man said with a twinkle in his eye. "Allow me to introduce myself. My name is Albert Cheevers, and I'm the birthday boy's son."

Albert pulled a beautiful silver case engraved with his initials out of his breast pocket. He opened it carefully and presented Robert with his business card.

"I really would like to get to know you better. Please call my office to set up a meeting," he said. "Oh, one more thing: please take care of that beautiful mother of yours. My father is absolutely smitten!"

With that, Albert turned to rejoin the conga line.

2

The Mentor

A WEEK LATER, ROBERT STOOD on a downtown
sidewalk, looking up at the fifty-story tower where
Albert's office was located. The building was archi-
tecturally stunning, built of green-tinted glass with a
sandstone pyramid that seemed to float on top.

The Cheevers family, which owned the building
and other sizeable commercial real estate properties,
used the pyramid as the headquarters for its wealth
management company and family foundation. Robert
remembered visiting the building when he started
writing key officer insurance. But he had never suc-
ceeded in getting past the stern receptionist on the top
floor where the high-level executives worked.

Robert hurried through a lobby filled with con-
temporary art and made his way to the building's
central bank of elevators. Within seconds, the elevator reserved for the forty-fifth to fiftieth floors, which
Cheevers Capital Management occupied, opened, and
Robert stepped inside.

As the elevator ascended, Robert noticed framed
images displayed in the elevator. The photos high-
lighted racially diverse groups of children playing

and studying together—a visual reminder that the Cheevers Charitable Foundation was one of the largest supporters of local schools.

Robert was so engrossed in the pictures that he lingered for a few seconds after the elevator doors opened. When he felt that somebody was looking at him, he stepped out—and found himself standing in front of a smiling receptionist seated behind a futuristic wood desk with a floating glass top.

"Welcome, Mr. Hanson," she said. She stood up and gestured, directing him toward a set of tall red double doors. "Mr. Cheevers is expecting you."

Entering the executive suite, Robert immediately felt queasy. What looked to be a sandstone pyramid from street level was actually made of tinted glass. As he drew closer, he felt as if he were nearing the edge of a cliff.

"Amazing, isn't it?" Albert was standing in front of a large desk at the window's edge. He pointed Robert toward two modern black leather sofas facing one another in the middle of the room. "I'm sorry that we didn't have time to talk the other night. But I'm all ears now."

Albert's friendly manner immediately put Robert at ease. Having pent up his feelings for so long, Robert was relieved to finally be able to share his fears that he might lose his home and business. Albert listened closely while nodding his head in sympathy.

Winding down his monologue, Robert concluded, "The big insurance companies have so much more money to spend on marketing than we do. Their relentless focus on low premiums has convinced many of our long-term clients to switch over to them. Sometimes I wonder whether we can compete."

"You're definitely in a tough spot," Albert said. "I have an idea of what you might be feeling, because I once doubted whether I could keep our company going through tough times. When I became company president, we lost many clients who felt loyal to my father but not to me. Honestly, I couldn't blame them. Even though I had worked with Dad for more than twenty years, most clients had no contact with me, since I was happy to be a numbers guy who kept in the background.

"Luckily, Dad helped me overcome my doubts and habits. He assured me that if I simply focused on building strong connections, our clients not only would stay loyal but would also refer people to our business. He was absolutely right."

Robert nodded as Albert spoke. Yet it was hard for him to disguise his doubt that such a simple idea could make such a big impact—and he could see that Albert saw his skepticism.

Albert said, "Look, if you'd like, I'd be glad to introduce you to the best relationship builders I know. After you've seen them in action, I'm sure that you'll see many new possibilities for your agency."

"The sooner, the better," said Robert.

3

Wake Me Up

THE STRONG SMELL OF freshly brewed coffee wafting out into the parking lot of Fuller's Café put a smile on Robert's face and fueled his appetite. He had never been to Fuller's, although it was located on one of the city's busiest streets. He had never paid the café much attention as he sped past on his way to work.

As he walked across the parking lot, he noticed some unusual details. Unlike many downtown parking lots, this one was immaculate. A teenage boy in a starched white shirt and black slacks was sweeping vigorously. "Welcome to Fuller's," the boy said, catching Robert's eye.

"Thank you. You're energetic for so early in the morning."

The boy laughed. "I'm just getting things ready for the most important people in the world."

The café itself was a 1950s-style diner with a horseshoe counter at the center and six red-upholstered booths along the walls. Robert asked a matronly-looking woman with grey-streaked hair knotted up in a bun whether he could take one of the booths as he waited for his friend to arrive.

"Of course, hon," she said. "Please make yourself at home. I'll be right with you."

Before taking a seat, Robert noticed a stack of newspapers with the typical array of depressing headlines: persistent high unemployment, a devastating apartment fire, and the rising national crime rate.

Looking around for something more uplifting to read, he noticed a small bookcase in a corner with a small handwritten sign on top: "Fuller's Café Little Free Library. Please take a book and leave one that inspired you."

Robert picked up a dog-eared copy of Frank Bettger's motivational classic *How I Raised Myself from Failure to Success in Selling*. He took it to a booth to read while he waited for Albert. As engrossed as he was in the story of a realtor who rose from rags to riches, Robert couldn't help but notice that the woman who had greeted him stepped briskly to the entrance with a smile whenever someone new entered the café.

She gave each of them a hug, asking about their families and their health. To some, she inquired why it had been so long since they last stopped in. She listened closely and asked thoughtful questions in response. It struck Robert that she really cared about each and every customer.

She approached Robert's booth with a pot of coffee. "So sorry it took me so long to get back to you, but I wanted to be sure I could offer you fresh-brewed coffee. We're slammed this morning. But here's a little treat for you while you wait for your friend."

With a wink, she placed three espresso beans covered in dark chocolate on the dish next to Robert's coffee mug. She then filled the mug to the brim and left the coffee pot on the table before scurrying off to greet a new arrival.

Robert watched closely as she worked her way around the room, chatting with customers, laughing at their jokes, and doling out chocolate-covered espresso beans with every cup she poured. She brought such joy to everything that she did that her customers couldn't help but smile.

"Enjoying your first lesson?" Albert asked as he approached Robert from behind. "Isn't Janice remarkable? I've paid a fortune to bring customer service trainers into our company, but it has proven much more effective to bring employees to Fuller's Café so they can see Janice in action. She has such a gift for making all her customers feel special."

At that moment, Janice came over to the table. "Good morning, handsome," she said to Albert with a grin. "The usual?"

"Please," Albert said. "And bring one for my friend Robert as well."

Robert wasn't sure, but he could have sworn that Janice communicated the order back to the kitchen in a little song. He heard the sound of chopping and the loud whirring of a blender. Soon, Janice came to the table with two giant milkshake glasses full of a thick dark-green concoction.

Albert eagerly brought the drink to his lips. Robert,

on the other hand, eyed the beverage warily. His face must have communicated his concern, because Albert put down his glass and began to tell Robert about the origin of the "Wake Me Up Smoothie," as it was called on the menu.

"A few months ago, I felt sluggish and tired," Albert said. "Janice knew me well enough to know that I was ready for a healthy change. So she began experimenting until she came up with the perfect nutrient-rich smoothie. It's now a permanent part of the café menu and my diet."

Albert shared that since he began drinking the healthy green smoothies he had dropped twenty-five pounds and had more energy than ever. With his curiosity now piqued, Robert picked up the smoothie and took a delicate sip. It was surprisingly tasty.

As the two men talked, Janice continued to circulate around the restaurant refilling coffee cups and making each customer feel like the most important person in the world.

"I'm learning so much about customer service just from watching Janice in action," Robert said.

"I'm glad," smiled Albert. "But, we've only just started. Your head will really be spinning with possibilities for your agency when you see what else I have in store for you. How about coming by my office at 8:00 AM tomorrow?"

"I can't wait!"

4

ROBERT ARRIVED AT HIS insurance agency deter-mined to do things differently. Watching how Janice treated her diners like family made him realize that he and the rest of his staff were not taking enough time to connect with people—including each other.

Instead of rushing through the front door as usual, Robert stopped at the front desk. "Morning, May. How's it going?"

She was clearly surprised: Robert normally was so engrossed in his smartphone, reading emails and text messages, that he would barely acknowledge her as he passed by.

"I'm pretty good," May said. "Now, if I could only kick this cold. It's been hanging on for weeks!"

"If you want to get better quickly, you need to go to Fuller's Café and try one of their green smoothies. I had my first one today, and I feel like a new man. They really work!"

May didn't know what was in those green smoothies, but she hoped that Robert kept drinking them. She couldn't remember ever having seen him so upbeat.

In his office, Robert checked his email and was

thrilled to see that his accountant, Stan Friedman, had referred the CFO at a large company. Typically, when Robert received a referral, he would send an email introducing himself and try to schedule a meeting with the prospect. He would usually thank the person making the referral with a quick text or email, but it was almost always an afterthought, and sometimes he would forget to do it.

Remembering how Janice connected with her diners in personal ways, Robert decided to try a different tack. He picked up the phone.

"Hey Stan! Robert here. Thanks so much for referring Jim. He seems like a great prospect. Your referrals really mean a lot to me."

There was a brief silence. Stan had known Robert for twenty years, but he couldn't remember ever having received a call from him thanking him for a referral.

"How are you and your wife doing?" Robert continued. He knew that Stan's wife had been going through treatment for breast cancer.

"Well, things are looking a bit better now," Stan said. "But recovering from the side effects of chemo has been a lot harder than we expected."

"I'm very sorry to hear that," Robert said. "I remember how rough chemo was for my mother."

They talked about personal matters for about fifteen minutes; then Stan shifted the conversation to business. He said Jim Hedges was one of his best clients, and fast-rising insurance premiums were contributing to the declining profitability of Jim's business. He concluded, "Jim is looking for some solid insurance solutions. Of course, I thought of you."

Robert thanked Stan again and hung up the phone. He immediately went online and ordered a bouquet of fresh flowers for Stan's wife. This simple act of kindness made him feel great—even better than the business referral he had received from Stan.

That night, when he got home, Robert gave his wife a kiss and big hug. Instead of rushing into the living room to read the newspaper and drink his customary gin and tonic, he sat on a barstool in the kitchen where Marion was grating parmesan cheese for a pasta Bolognese dinner. He listened attentively as she described a disagreement she'd had that day with her boss, and he empathized with her frustration.

Usually, when Marion shared her workplace frustrations, Robert cut her off to suggest solutions. However, having experienced how conscious listening had helped him connect better with May and Stan, he decided to try the same approach at home.

Marion had no idea what had caused Robert's sudden change in behavior, but she hoped that it would continue.

5

A Jolt

A LOUD BOOM IN THE middle of the night jolted Robert and Marion awake. The house groaned as if a giant had stepped on it. Their initial thought was that a car had crashed into the downstairs living room. Hearing a loud shriek coming from their twenty-six-year-old daughter's room, they jumped out of bed and rushed down the hallway.

They found Andrea sitting up in bed, terrified. A small gash on her forehead was the only visible sign of injury. This was amazing, considering that a powerful wind gust had wrenched a massive branch from the ten-story-tall Douglas fir tree in the backyard. It had fallen through the roof and into the middle of Andrea's room which she had recently moved back into so she could save up money for a down payment on a condo.

After calming Andrea and moving her to the downstairs sofa, Robert and Marion returned to their bedroom. It seemed that nothing could be done about the branch and the roof at that late hour; fortunately, the weather had calmed.

Unable to sleep with so much adrenaline pumping through his body, Robert padded quietly to his downstairs office. He texted Albert to explain that he would be unable to meet the next day as planned. He then headed back to bed to get a couple of hours of sleep.

A text message from Albert was waiting when Robert awoke: "Relieved that all of you are ok! Call Terry Jones of Treeology. He can help with cleanup."

Robert found Treeology's website and clicked on the video on the home page. It showed Terry standing next to a beautiful Japanese maple. He explained how as a child he had climbed all the trees in his neighborhood and how lucky he was to climb trees for a living. As Terry spoke, images of happy customers and their testimonials scrolled across the screen. Robert opened the company blog, which featured many helpful articles about tree care.

Convinced of Treeology's expertise, Robert called Terry, who picked up after just two rings. Robert explained the fallen branch and the damage to the house.

"Wow, that sounds like a close call! You're incredibly lucky that nobody got hurt," Terry said with genuine concern.

A few hours later, Robert heard rattling as a large green pickup truck with extension ladders mounted on each side pulled into the driveway. Out jumped Terry, a bit over five feet tall with tightly cropped blond hair and an athletic build well-suited for tree climbing.

Terry shook Robert's hand firmly while looking up

at the branch protruding from the roof. "That's an impressive souvenir you have there," he said.

Terry got to work immediately. He walked around the base of the tree from which the branch fell and dug into the dirt to inspect the roots. Then he went back to the truck to grab ropes and pulleys. Robert watched in amazement as Terry quickly ascended to the midpoint of the tree to study where the two main branches split off from the trunk.

Using a winch, Terry removed the fallen tree branch from the roof and placed a plastic tarp over a gaping hole about five feet wide by eight feet long.

When Terry dropped to the ground, Robert was waiting. He was anxious to learn whether the next big storm might topple the entire tree onto his or one of his neighbors' homes. Terry was quick to reassure him.

"For a Douglas fir, your tree is relatively young at about one hundred and fifty years old. It appears to have a strong root system and is in no imminent danger of falling. In fact, it should be standing here well after our great-grandchildren have walked the earth—trees like this one commonly live five hundred years or more."

Terry recommended thinning out the dead branches to reduce the impact of wind pushing against the tree and referred Robert to articles on his website that described the ins and outs of pruning a Douglas fir. He also offered to put Robert on the list for his monthly newsletter that provided tree care and gardening information.

"I'll send my crew by later this morning to board up the hole until your roof can be permanently fixed, but the tarp should do for now."

Grateful, Robert invited Terry into the house for a cup of coffee and some of Marion's peanut butter cookies. Taking a seat across from Terry at the kitchen table, Robert asked him, "How long have you known Albert?"

"Hmmm. It must be about ten years now. That makes him a fairly new customer. Most folks have been with us for twenty years or more."

Impressed, Robert asked Terry his secret for keeping customers so long.

"It's pretty simple, actually. I'm a tree teacher first and a tree trimmer second."

"What do you mean by that?"

Terry explained that many of his large competitors didn't see much value in sharing their knowledge with customers. Instead, they tried to win market share with advertising and discounting. In contrast, he believed it was much more important to educate customers and provide stellar service. He was convinced that this approach had helped Treeology become one of the most successful local tree care companies.

"I also have learned how important it is to be open to new ideas, because the ways that consumers gather information and make decisions are constantly changing."

He explained that Treeology's communications improved dramatically when his son Adam joined the family business. One of Adam's first actions was to create a monthly e-newsletter to teach customers how to care for their trees and create beautiful outdoor spaces.

"Every time we finish a job for a new customer, we ask whether they'd like to get our e-newsletter," Terry said. "Our first edition went out to about forty family members and friends. Today, around six thousand people receive it every month. Our referrals go up every time we send one out, since it keeps us top of mind."

Robert continued with marketing-related questions, and Terry, who clearly loved helping his customers any way he could, explained that his company's videos and blog posts were also highly effective at generating leads and keeping the business on the first page of search engine results. His son kept close tabs on their online analytics, so Terry understood what kind of information attracted website visitors and *exactly* how they found his business.

Robert's mind was spinning with possibilities. If a small business like Treeology could adapt its style of communication to the needs and wants of its customers, why couldn't Hanson Insurance Agency do the same?

6

Ringing Ideas

ROBERT WAS SO EXCITED to talk with his employees about new marketing ideas that he sped right past two men in Santa hats ringing handbells on a corner just a couple of blocks from his office.

Having never seen bell ringers in the neighborhood, Robert glanced in his rearview mirror and noticed that one of the men had distinctive curly grey hair like Albert's poking out from underneath his hat. He made a quick U-turn to investigate.

"Hey there!" Albert said as Robert rolled down his window. "I'm surprised to see you here after what happened last night."

Robert smiled. "I wasn't planning on coming to work. But your tree guy fired me up with so many great ideas that I just couldn't wait to share them with my team."

"I'm not surprised," Albert said. "Terry is one of the brightest business guys I know. If you have a minute, why don't you get out of the car so I can introduce you to my friend Scott Boyle?"

Scott's name sounded familiar to Robert, and his face looked familiar too, yet he couldn't quite place him. He found a parking spot and walked back to join them.

"How long have you both been out here?" Robert asked.

"About two hours, I think," Albert said. "But time really flies when I'm with Scott."

Robert asked how their donations were going. He expected to hear that they had collected very little, as they were in an economically depressed neighborhood.

"We're certainly off to a good start," Scott replied. "We've already had about $2,500 in donations—and the bank will match whatever we raise."

A light bulb went off in Robert's head: he was speaking with Scott Boyle, whose family had founded First City Bank. But he wondered why Scott and Albert were ringing bells on a cold winter day.

As if he had read Robert's mind, Scott continued, "As a kid, I rang bells with my dad every year, just as he had done with his father. In fact, my grandfather started bell ringing because he wanted to do something for people struggling during the Great Depression. Soon, my grandfather's employees joined in. Over the past eighty years, most of our employees have volunteered as holiday bell ringers—and many have done so every year for decades."

A car horn interrupted their conversation. Scott hurried out into the street as the window of a black luxury sedan slowly rolled down. A well-dressed man reached out with five crisp one-hundred-dollar bills. "Merry Christmas, Scott! Thanks for what you're doing."

Scott rejoined Albert and Robert. "That guy sells the financial software that our bank uses," he explained. "I always let our vendors know where I'll be ringing bells. My employees do the same with their friends and family members. You'd be surprised at how many people will contribute to a worthy cause when you ask."

Albert nodded. "I used to just put money in Scott's bucket. But when I saw how much fun he and his employees were having, I just had to join them. Now I wouldn't miss this holiday tradition for anything."

As Albert spoke, Robert noticed an old man on the other side of the street. He was pushing a shopping cart full of bottles for recycling. "How's it going, Jack?" Scott called out. The recycler looked up and smiled a wide toothless grin before crossing the street to drop a handful of hard-earned quarters into Scott's bucket.

7

Commitment to Change

THE FAINT SOUND OF ringing bells could still be heard a few blocks away at Hanson Insurance Agency, where eight employees were seated around a dark oval conference table. Antique sepia-tone photos dating back to when the business was established in the 1920s graced the wood-paneled walls.

Everybody knew that the agency was in trouble. There was a general sense of foreboding that Robert had called the meeting to announce a layoff. When he strode into the room, a few anxious employees inhaled sharply. They expected the worst.

"As you know, the past few years have been challenging," Robert began. People exchanged knowing looks, and a few nervously clenched their fists.

"I appreciate how hard everybody has been working," he continued. "But working hard isn't enough. We need to embrace the wisdom of Henry Ford, who said 'If you always do what you've always done, you'll always get what you've always got.' In our case, we need to get much better at building relationships with our clients so they stay with us and refer others. I've been learning how we can do this much better."

Robert's optimism immediately lifted people's spirits. He continued, "I know it is easy to get bogged down in the technical details of the policies that we sell and the claims we process. But when we do that, we lose touch with the human side of our business.

"A few days ago, I saw Janice, a server at Fuller's Café on Beacon Street, in action. I watched her make a personal connection with *every single person* in the restaurant even though she was waiting on a roomful of tables all by herself."

Hearing Janice's name, a couple of employees smiled in recognition.

Insurance agent Rick Payton spoke up. "When I go to Fuller's, Janice makes me feel like I'm sitting at my mom's breakfast table. Her hospitality is amazing."

A few others nodded. Yet a vibe of skepticism emanated from one person. Peter Constanza, who had been with the agency for twenty-three years and was counting the days until retirement, leaned over and whispered to the newest employee, Sam Hales: *"The boss is really grasping at straws. I can't believe that he's getting business ideas from a waitress."*

Not hearing Peter, Robert continued: "As most of you know, our family had a close call last night when a branch smashed through our roof. Not only was it a reminder about the importance of the insurance policies we sell, but it was a great business lesson, too. The tree guy who came to clean things up and inspect our tree told me how his company is building strong customer relationships that are fueling success."

As Robert shared the lessons he had learned from Terry, Peter rolled his eyes and arched an eyebrow at Sam. Meanwhile, Robert's daughter Andrea, who had been working at the agency with her father since graduating from college five years ago, scribbled notes as fast as she could. She was excited to hear her father embracing ideas similar to ones that she had been thinking about for months.

8

AFTER THE STAFF MEETING, Robert returned to his office with a lightness in his step that he hadn't felt in years. But as he sank back into his high-backed leather office chair, a wave of exhaustion overcame him from the interrupted sleep of the night before. He closed his eyes for a nap.

He awoke twenty-five minutes later feeling refreshed and focused. Curious to learn about Scott Boyle's bell ringing activities, he began searching online. One of the first results was a cover story from the town's local newspaper. Below a photo of a smiling Scott, Robert read:

> For 80 years, the Boyle family has been a December presence on city streets. Scott Boyle, president of First City Bank, and seventy-five of the bank's employees have been ringing bells for charity since Thanksgiving. Tim McCarthy, regional vice president of All Hands Together, a homeless shelter, said, "Without the fundraising of the Boyles and First City employees, we

couldn't feed all the people who depend on us, especially during the cold weather."

The second search result was another story in the local business newspaper that focused on First City Bank's steady growth, even during the recent economic downturn.

While many community banks have lost market share to large national competitors with massive advertising budgets, First City Bank has shown steady growth over the past decade. Satisfaction surveys show that customers give the bank high marks for outstanding service as well as its charitable activities such as its annual holiday bell ringing campaign.

Robert thought about how his insurance agency had moved away from activities that supported the community. Ten years ago, the agency had sponsored a local Little League team, bought tables at non-profit fundraising events, and matched employees' charitable donations. When the recession hit, however, Robert had felt forced to halt the agency's give-back activities, and he had never resumed them.

As Robert contemplated ways to reengage the agency in the community and get back on a philanthropic track, he got a call from Albert.

"Thanks for stopping by this morning. Scott told me he'd have liked more time to chat with you. Can you join us tomorrow for our Rotary Club luncheon downtown?"

Robert had been invited to attend many Rotary meetings over the years, but ever since he attended just one meeting with his father, his answer had been a consistent "no." In spite of various friends in Rotary encouraging him to attend meetings, he felt he couldn't take time out of his busy schedule. Since the invitation was from Albert, however, Robert accepted without hesitation.

After hanging up, Robert stopped by Andrea's desk to offer her a ride home. On her screen was a picture of Alice, a customer service representative at the agency for the past twenty-five years. Andrea was writing up an interview in a Q&A format.

"What are you working on?" asked Robert.

"Well, after hearing you rave so much about Terry's e-newsletter, I thought we should start our own. I've already written an article about umbrella insurance coverage; that's an important topic. But I also wanted to give people a sense of who we are, so I decided to do this interview with Alice. What do you think?"

As Robert read the article onscreen, he was surprised to learn things about Alice that he had never known. Not only was Alice a volunteer for multiple community organizations, but she also was an editor for a website that covered fun and interesting things to do in the area.

Alice was not alone in giving back to the community. Many of her colleagues were volunteers in non-profit organizations, active in service clubs and religious institutions, and PTA leaders. Together, they made Hanson Insurance Agency stand apart from many big insurance companies that had few employees living and volunteering in the community.

"What do you think?" Andrea asked.

"That we should have been sharing great stories like this many years ago," Robert replied.

9

Membership Advantages

WALKING INTO THE ORNATE marble-walled lobby of the Regal Hotel, where the Downtown Rotary Club had held its weekly Tuesday lunch meeting for the past fifty years, Robert felt as if he had stepped back into time. He imagined that he would soon be shaking hands with serious-looking men in suits, just like when he attended his last meeting twenty years earlier.

When he arrived at the elegant dining room, Robert thought he was in the wrong place. Most of the three hundred people in attendance were dressed in casual business attire. About a third of attendees were women. And more than half looked to be under forty years old.

He noticed Albert waving at him from a corner of the ballroom. Robert felt an immediate sense of relief, as he always felt uncomfortable in a roomful of strangers. He wound his way through clusters of people in animated conversations to join Albert and Scott.

"I'm glad you could make it," Albert said, clapping Robert on the back. "Let's grab some lunch right away—we're starving."

As they waited for food, Robert said, "Your club is

sure different from what I expected. When I last visited Rotary twenty years ago, it was all white—and all men. Also, it might just be that I'm getting older, but it seems like there are more young people than I remember."

Scott laughed. "I'm with you. I keep telling people that we're not getting older; it's just that everyone else is getting younger!"

Scott explained that the club's diversity was reflected in its leadership over the past few years. Three of the last five club presidents had been women or minorities. Diversity in club leadership had helped it attract diverse members over the past decade.

"Speaking of new people, let's go meet some," said Albert, steering Scott and Robert toward a table with eight place settings; three women were already sitting there.

Albert said, "Hi! Mind if we join you?"

An African American woman in her mid-thirties smiled. "Please, have a seat. I'm Abby Richards. Nice to meet you."

Taking a seat next to Abby, Robert introduced himself and asked, "How long have you been in Rotary?"

"I've been a member of this club for about four years. Before that I had a Rotary Scholarship to do a year of graduate studies in Australia."

Robert, who had left the country only once to visit Canada, was fascinated. "What was living in Australia like?"

"Do you have a few hours?" Abby laughed. "It truly was one of the most amazing experiences of my life."

She explained that she hadn't been quite sure what to expect before going to Australia. She was delighted to find that nearly everybody she met was warm and kind.

"At first, I thought that I received special treatment since I was a foreigner. But everyone treated each other with extraordinary kindness. It was such an eye-opening experience."

Jumping into the conversation, Albert said, "I'm not surprised. I was lucky enough to go to Australia a couple of years ago for the Rotary International Convention in Sydney. The Australian Rotarians were incredibly welcoming. It's definitely one of the friendliest places I've ever visited. All this talk about travel makes me want to pack my bags and go somewhere interesting."

Scott said, "Well, you're in luck. Abby runs a travel concierge business. She arranged an incredible three-week trip to South America for my wife and me last year."

"Isn't Rotary terrific?" Abby said laughing. "I get to talk about fun things—and a fellow Rotarian sells my services!"

The club president called the meeting to order. During the hour-long program, Robert learned about many worthwhile community service projects that the club sponsored locally and internationally. Although the program was interesting, Robert found it hard to stay focused on what was being said, as the conversation with Abby had him daydreaming about taking a vacation with his wife—something they hadn't done in years.

Robert's daydream caused him to momentarily push his financial worries aside. When the meeting adjourned, Robert gave Abby his card and said, "So great meeting you. Can I stop by your office sometime soon? I would like your help planning a surprise vacation for my wife."

"I'd be glad to help," Abby replied. "I work from my home office, so how about meeting at the Travel Café next Monday morning—say, at 10?"

After confirming the meeting, Robert joined Scott and Albert, who suggested that they take the stairs down to the parking garage. Albert said he was always looking for opportunities to exercise, as he was convinced that one of his father's longevity secrets was to simply keep moving.

Walking down the stairs, Robert couldn't hide his enthusiasm. "What a great meeting! The timing couldn't have been better. I've wanted to surprise Marion with a trip for quite some time now, and Abby seems like the perfect person to help. Out of curiosity, how much business do you think she gets from being a Rotarian?"

"Quite a lot, I'm sure," Scott said. "Last week I sat next to our club president, Jim Miller. We had a conversation about how much Rotary has helped our businesses over the years. Jim told me that about a quarter of his business now comes from Rotary members and their referrals."

"That's amazing. Is Jim's success typical?"

Albert responded, "It's not unusual for a committed Rotarian, but it takes time. I've been a Rotarian for nearly thirty years, and Dad was a club member for fifty years before he retired. I'm guessing that about twenty percent of our clients come from connections that we've made at Rotary over the years."

"But I didn't notice anybody exchanging leads like I've seen at other business meetings," Robert said.

"Well, Rotary is different from business groups that encourage members to pass leads to one another," Albert said. "We focus on 'Service Above Self.' As Rotarians, we have many opportunities to get involved in Rotary service projects in our communities and overseas. By doing this, we make connections that result in wonderful friendships. And some of the friends we make in Rotary turn out to be valuable business connections, too."

For Robert, the message was clear: like everyone, Rotarians prefer to do business with people they *know, like,* and *trust.* Seeing one another on a weekly basis and working together on service projects, Rotary Club members have an opportunity to develop deep relationships. And when it came time to choose who to do business with, it was only natural that Rotarians sought out fellow club members.

10

Deliver Value

LOOK AT THOSE THREE-HUNDRED-YEAR-OLD buildings and cobblestone streets. I sure wish I could visit Germany again!"

Robert had come home from the office to find Marion engrossed in a television show. He sat down on the sofa next to her and watched as the show's host guided viewers on a trip through the Bavarian countryside.

Growing up, Marion had travelled to Germany every summer with her parents to visit her German grandparents, aunts, uncles, and cousins. Those trips were the happiest memories of her childhood, and she often longed to return.

"We'll go there together, I promise," Robert said affectionately. At the same time, he felt guilty for holding out hope for such a trip when their financial situation was so precarious.

That night, Robert lay in bed thinking about everything he had learned about building better business relationships. He knew that he should start writing things down so he could start acting on so many good ideas. But sleep overtook him before he could get out of bed.

He woke to the sweet smell of German apple pancakes—one of Marion's favorite dishes. He dressed hurriedly, knowing that he needed to speed things along to arrive on time for his meeting with Abby.

Marion was at the stovetop, spatula in hand. "Good morning," he greeted her with a kiss. "I'm sorry that I can't eat with you and Andrea. Your pancakes smell amazing as usual."

"Watching that television show last night inspired me to cook these," Marion said.

"Can I take a rain check?"

"Of course." Marion kissed him on the cheek. He headed out the door, thinking about fluffy pancakes with warm apple slices, melted butter, and hot maple syrup.

Arriving at the Travel Café, Robert spotted Abby working on her laptop. He waved, but she didn't see him. As he made his way over to her table, he noticed that she was smiling.

"Hi Abby," Robert said. "I hope I'm not interrupting something important."

Abby looked up with a big smile. "Wonderful to see you! I'm just putting the finishing touches on a greeting card."

On Abby's laptop screen, Robert saw two photos. One was of her with another woman, both wearing fancy evening dresses, standing in the lobby of a luxury hotel. The other was of a tropical beach, empty except for an umbrella and a chair. Underneath both photos, Abby had typed a note, using a computer font that looked like handwriting.

"Last night, I attended a charity auction for my son's elementary school," Abby explained. "At the event, I spoke with Janet, who you see in this photo. She serves on the PTA with me. During the dinner, she told me she wants to organize a family trip to Australia over Christmas break but hasn't had time to do so. So I'm creating a greeting card with a picture of us at the event, a photo of my favorite Australian beach, and a message telling Janet how much I enjoyed our conversation and how I would be glad to help plan her family's trip to Australia."

Robert was impressed. "That's very thoughtful. But that seems like a lot of effort."

"It's not really. In this case, I'm using an online card service that lets me upload my own photos and uses my personal handwriting font. The company then prints and mails the card for me. But I also send many handwritten notes—and I always have a stack of cards on hand!"

Robert was impressed. He couldn't remember the last time he'd received a personal greeting card in the mail, outside of Christmas. Yet he asked, "Aren't cards a bit old-fashioned for business?"

"That's just the point!" Abby said. "People are so bombarded with information that they tend to ignore email and social media messages. But I know from experience that the personal cards I mail always get opened and make an impact. People let me know!"

She continued, "I used to send out hundreds of emails introducing my services to HR departments and sales managers at companies that book corporate travel. Those messages didn't set me apart or help me get much business. Most were probably deleted before they got read.

"Now I focus on making meaningful connections with people in the real world, and I follow up with personal cards to help develop relationships."

Abby related how she would visit people at their offices and see that they still had cards she sent them years ago on display. "Personal greeting cards are my secret weapon for generating repeat and referred business!"

"I would be interested in having my team give your approach a try," Robert said. "In fact, I would love to have you come to one of our staff meetings and explain what you're doing. But I need your help with something else first."

Robert shared his wife's dream of vacationing in Germany—the places she wanted to visit and the types of food and accommodations she liked.

"Well, you've given me plenty of information to plan a great itinerary," Abby said. "You should plan at least a two-week trip, so you have enough time to visit all the places on your wife's list without feeling too rushed. Also, she has great taste: you've described a five-star experience. I'm guessing that with airfare, hotels, ground transportation, and food, such a trip could easily run over ten thousand."

Robert winced and shook his head.

Reading his facial expression, Abby responded, "If going to Germany isn't viable now, there's an alternative worth considering." She began typing. Instantly, pictures of Bavarian-style houses began popping up. Only these weren't in Germany, but in a town three hundred miles away, built in an authentic Bavarian style.

Abby reassured Robert that the town wasn't a kitschy tourist trap. "I was there last year and enjoyed great hiking and biking trails and lots of German restaurants and interesting shops. It might be just the cure for your wife's nostalgia for Germany . . . and you can't beat the price."

"Sounds great," said Robert. "Can I have you handle the booking?"

"You could," Abby said. "But it would be less expensive if you made arrangements directly. I'm more than happy to recommend places to stay and eat as well as things to do."

Robert said, "I feel bad that I'm not paying you for anything—you work on commission, don't you?"

"Don't worry about me," said Abby. "My business is all about helping people have great trips, whether or not I earn a commission. From experience, I know that some will become paying clients and many will refer their friends, whether or not they book through me."

11

Surprise

"NOW ARE YOU GOING to tell me where we're going?" Marion asked as Robert opened the car door for her.

For the past week, Robert had been making arrangements for a surprise trip to celebrate their thirtieth wedding anniversary. As hard as Marion had tried, Robert had maintained total secrecy about their destination. The only thing he told her was to pack a suitcase for four days.

As they drove to the airport, Marion said she was sure they were going to Florida. To throw her off track, Robert had suggested that she pack a bathing suit, comfortable shoes, and casual clothing—to her, that seemed to suggest Key West, a place they had enjoyed many years ago.

The intrigue deepened as Robert drove past the airport exit. Marion didn't seem to mind, though—she was just happy that they were finally going on a vacation. She looked at Robert and smiled.

Three hours into the trip, Robert turned onto a winding mountain road and began fiddling with the radio. The car speakers crackled with static until weak strains of polka music grew louder. As the song ended, an announcer came on the air and delivered the weather forecast in flawless German.

Marion's eyes lit up. "That's it. We're going to Augsburg! I've heard so many great things from friends who've been there."

An hour later they turned onto a winding gravel road that led to a three-story home built in a sturdy Bavarian style, with solid wood beams and a white-washed exterior, decorated with baskets of fuchsias and other brightly colored flowers. Situated on the edge of a meadow, it had a gorgeous view of jagged granite peaks. It looked like it had been there for centuries.

Robert parked the car. As he and Marion stepped out into the crisp, early-evening air, a black-and-white Great Dane ambled over to greet them, wagging his long, skinny tail.

"I sure hope you're not afraid of dogs," a man called out from the front porch. The innkeeper was a wiry, middle-aged man with curly brown hair and a big grin. He stepped down briskly to greet them. "Welcome to the Alpine Inn. I'm Sam Johnson. I see that our canine ambassador Chuck has already welcomed you. Here, let me help you with your luggage."

Walking with Sam toward the house, Marion and Robert were surprised to find themselves dragging a bit, then realized it was the altitude change. Sam invited them to make themselves at home in the living room in front of the fireplace as he took their bags to their room.

The warm fire reinvigorated them, as did the herbal tea and homemade apple strudel that had been laid out on the coffee table. Returning with a clipboard, Sam took a seat across from the Hansons.

"There's so much to do in Augsburg," he began. "But it's also a wonderful place for simply relaxing. If you're not too tired, I'd be happy to provide some recommendations."

Sam had grown up in Augsburg and knew the town inside and out. Marion and Robert listened closely as he gave them a rundown of the area's biking and hiking trails. He told them where to find the best German food and suggested places to listen to polka music— and dance, if they felt like it.

When Robert and Marion both yawned, Sam stopped. "Sorry if I've exhausted you. Once I get going on what to do here, I'm hard to shut off. Just one more thing. What would you like for breakfast?" Sam pointed to a blackboard near the kitchen door. It featured a mouthwatering menu of items both savory and sweet. They made their selections and retired to their room for an early bedtime.

Over the next three days, the Hansons spent most of their time hiking along the narrow forest paths that surrounded the town. It had been years since they had hiked together, and the fresh air and exercise energized them. They spent the evenings chatting in front of a crackling fire in the cozy living room that they had all to themselves.

The night before their departure, after Marion had turned in early to read in bed, Grace, Sam's wife and co-owner of the inn, came into the living room where Robert was reading.

"How about a nightcap?" she asked. "I have a fresh batch of chocolate chip cookies coming out of the oven in just a few minutes. They go well with a glass of port."

Robert had been hoping for a chance to ask questions about the inn, as it had impressed him as being a very well-run business. In addition to the gourmet breakfasts, there had been many other thoughtful touches throughout their stay—from freshly baked pastries in the afternoon to a self-serve bar in the library with complimentary wine, beer, and soft drinks.

Grace returned with a tray of cookies and two glasses of ruby red port. After complimenting her on the cookies, Robert asked, "What inspired you and Sam to open this place?"

"Great question! We certainly had no grand plan for becoming innkeepers. In fact, we moved here so that Sam could retire early and go fishing. I wanted a change of pace and thought I'd sell country homes to city dwellers.

"Fortunately, after working twenty-five years as a realtor in the city, I had a book of clients who knew me well. I had helped some of them buy and sell multiple homes, and I stayed connected with them over the years through newsletters, personal visits, and small things like giving away free pies and other goodies for Thanksgiving and Valentine's Day."

Grace explained that many of her clients were interested in either retiring to the country or buying a vacation home. Yet there were few places for them to stay while they were in Augsburg on house-hunting visits. The only overnight options were second-rate budget hotels.

Hearing the conversation in the living room, Sam came in and sat on the loveseat next to Grace. "I thought that hanging out in retirement would be enough for me," he said. "But after a few months, I was bored silly. Grace's frustration in finding a place for her clients to stay really got me thinking about taking on a new challenge."

The Alpine Inn offered just the challenge he was seeking. Sam explained, "This place sure needed some attention. When we first saw it, the front yard was a jungle of weeds and there was paint peeling off of every surface, inside and out. Fortunately, the bones of the building were good. We knew that we could make it shine."

Marion, who had wandered into the living room looking for something to satisfy her sweet tooth, said, "It's hard to believe this place was ever neglected. It looks so beautiful now. We've just loved our time here."

Grace and Sam beamed. "Thank you very much," Sam said. "That means a lot to us. If it's not too much to ask, would you mind reviewing our place online? Our best marketing is the positive word of mouth we get from our guests. Seventy-five percent of our guests read online reviews before deciding to stay with us."

Sam explained that during their first few years in business, they were lucky to get great online reviews without asking. When they noticed that these reviews generated most of their bookings, they decided to always ask their guests during the checkout process.

"We've been delighted to find that our guests are happy to spread the good word about our business when we ask them," Sam said. "But we have to make it easy for them. We can't expect them to jump through hoops to post reviews."

Robert recalled how they had found the inn. "When I searched for hotels in Augsburg, your place came up at the top of search engine results. I was impressed that you had more reviews than any other property, including the large hotels."

"That's what I love to hear!" Sam practically jumped out of his chair with excitement. "We're at the top of search engines and travel websites for three reasons. First, we do everything possible to give our guests a reason to recommend us. Second, we let our guests know how much we appreciate them. And finally, we ask our guests to tell their friends about us and post reviews on their favorite websites."

Robert's mind was racing as he thought about how he could apply these simple principles to grow his insurance agency.

"Okay, okay," Marion said with a smile. "Enough about business. What is the last hike we should do tomorrow before heading home?"

12

Enthusiasm for Change

ROBERT PRACTICALLY BOUNCED THROUGH the doors of Hanson Insurance Agency on Monday morning. "Hi May! Beautiful day, isn't it?"

Not giving her a moment to respond, he continued, "We had a *fantastic* time in Augsburg. And I learned so many new things that will really help the agency. Please text everyone that we'll have a meeting in the conference room in two hours."

As the agency's employees gathered, it was clear that some were still nervous about losing their jobs. Robert quickly dispelled these fears with a smile.

"Good morning! I called this meeting to discuss the excellent business practices that I saw in action this past weekend. I'm convinced that better ways of doing business are essential for boosting our client loyalty and referrals."

"*Oh no, here he goes again,*" whispered Peter Constanza. The agency's cynic had once again seated himself next to new hire Sam Hales. "*Why does he think that so many of his personal experiences are relevant to how we do business?*"

Sam ignored Peter's whispering, as did Robert. Instead, Robert explained in detail the great customer service at the Alpine Inn and how its online customer reviews were helping to drive its success.

Andrea spoke up: "If we want online reviews, we need to focus on service. Many clients judge us more on how we make them feel than the policies that they buy. We're lucky to have May at the front desk. She's friendly with everybody, whether they're calling into the main number or walking into the office.

"But other points of contact are not nearly as impressive, including me at times. It's tough to sound as upbeat as May when the phone rings and interrupts my thoughts—especially when I haven't had my coffee!"

The others chuckled and nodded. Andrea concluded, "I bet each one of us can find ways to be more welcoming. Personally, I'm going to focus on being more enthusiastic when I'm interacting with clients and prospects."

Robert smiled. He was proud to hear Andrea share her thoughts so eloquently. He was also thrilled when other employees began to offer their ideas for improving service. The positive energy was contagious.

"We could stock snacks and drinks and offer them to clients visiting our office," Sam said. "It would make a positive first impression, just like the tea and apple strudel that you were offered when you checked in at the inn."

Even Bill Iverson, the agency's quiet IT manager, participated in the brainstorming. "I like the idea of asking for reviews. It has always bothered me that we have just a handful of online reviews while smaller agencies have dozens, and we've been around much longer than they have."

Nearly everybody in the room nodded. Bill continued, "When clients say good things about our agency, our producers and client service representatives need to see that moment as an opportunity to request an online review."

"Just a second," Peter interrupted. "I completely disagree. We're going to sound too pushy if we start begging people for reviews."

"I appreciate what you're saying," Bill said. "We definitely don't want to pressure anybody. But if we treat people right and let them know how grateful we are for their business, asking for a review is a natural next step. After all, it gives our clients an opportunity to help their friends, because they know that we'll treat them well."

Robert thanked everyone for their great ideas and brought the session to a close so he could get back to his office with a half hour to spare before a meeting he had scheduled with Albert. While the "old" Robert would have filled the time reading emails and surfing online, the "new" Robert chose a different course.

He had recently read about the positive benefits of meditation. Now, settling comfortably into a leather recliner in the corner of his office, Robert set the timer on his phone, leaned back, closed his eyes, and began to breathe deeply. He focused his thoughts on everything that was going well in his life and visualized what would improve in the future. He pictured his agency thriving, thanks to the loyalty and referrals of satisfied clients. When his mind began to wander, he concentrated on the many things that made him feel grateful.

Ten minutes later, the bell chimed on his phone. Robert felt energized and ready to put the many new ideas that he and his team had discussed into action.

13

The Art of Networking

COME JOIN US." ALBERT beckoned to Robert as he stepped out of the elevator onto the fiftieth floor.

Albert and a tall stranger were sitting across from each other on the black leather couches in the middle of Albert's office. "Robert, this is my old friend Charles Conerly," Albert said. "He owns CHG Commercial Real Estate. He's also the chairman of the chamber of commerce's board of directors."

Charles looked into Robert's eyes as he shook his hand with a firm grip. "Nice to meet you. When Albert told me that we would meet, I looked you up in the chamber's database and saw that your agency was a member for twenty-five years. I'm curious, though. Why did you drop your membership five years ago?"

Robert explained that he was forced to cut expenses when the recession hit. "I appreciate the lobbying that the chamber does for small businesses. But I just couldn't justify renewing our membership because I wasn't seeing a bottom-line benefit."

Albert countered with his own experience. "I understand the need for ROI as much as anybody. That's why our firm has been a chamber member for nearly fifty years. The chamber has provided so many great opportunities to build relationships that have led to some of our best clients."

Charles chuckled. "Thanks for that glowing testimonial, Albert. I can always count on you to be one of our most eloquent evangelists."

He turned his attention back to Robert. "I absolutely understand your concerns. In fact, I almost dropped out of the chamber myself ten years ago when I felt membership wasn't doing much for our business."

"So, why didn't you?" Robert asked.

"A friend who also belonged to the chamber pointed out some things that really shifted my thinking. He reminded me that I was not very involved in the chamber beyond attending an occasional business mixer. He also said that when I *did* show up for an event, I usually hung out with people I already knew."

Charles explained that, with his friend's encouragement, he had joined a few committees and volunteered to chair one of them. He'd also challenged himself to meet at least three new people at every chamber event.

"Making an effort to meet new people and stepping into a leadership role made all the difference. As chamber members got to know me better, they began to seek me out to help them with their commercial real estate needs. If I had quit the chamber before becoming truly engaged, I would have missed out on many great friendships and business opportunities."

Albert glanced at the clock. "Time to get moving, gentlemen," he said. "The mixer started thirty minutes ago, and I want to get there before the sharks devour all the shrimp on the buffet table." Robert and Charles laughed.

They took the elevator down to the mezzanine where the chamber had its office. The monthly business mixer was held in the building's large indoor atrium. As they joined a crowd of people milling around holding drinks and small plates of food, Robert took a deep breath. Networking always made him feel uncomfortable.

Albert glanced over at Robert and noticed his nervousness. "Stick with me and we'll have some fun!"

Someone was waving at Albert from across the room. "Follow me," he said to Robert. "I'm going to introduce you to my mortgage broker, Mike."

Albert strode across the room with Robert close behind. "Hey Mike! How's the family? Is Jill enjoying the first grade?"

"The family is doing great," Mike said. "Thanks for asking. Jill loves the first grade. By the way, your memory continues to amaze me."

Albert laughed. "I appreciate the kind words. Speaking of memory, before I forget, let me introduce you to Robert Hanson. You might know Robert's company. It's one of the oldest family-owned businesses in town. Robert's great-grandfather started it ninety-three years ago. Robert has helped companies like yours save a lot of money over the years with great insurance advice."

"Coming from a savvy businessman like Albert,

that's quite a compliment," Mike told Robert. "We should meet sometime soon so I can learn how you work. I'm always on the lookout for good insurance agents. Many of my clients have insurance needs."

Albert continued to lead Robert around the room, introducing him to people with genuine enthusiasm. Robert noted that Albert always started a conversation with at least a few personal questions or observations before mentioning anything about business. He admired Albert's ease at remembering names and building rapport.

Waiting in the buffet line, Robert asked Albert, "How do you remember so many names and details? I don't know anybody else who can do that."

"It's really not hard. I use the power of visualization. I associate names with physical objects and stories. For instance, the first time I met Mike, he told me great stories about his daughter Jill. While I certainly won't win any prizes for creativity, I associate Mike's name with a microphone. I'll never forget Mike or Jill's names because I imagine a microphone walking up the hill with Jill to fetch a pail of water."

The image made Robert laugh out loud. "I know it sounds strange," Albert said. "But once you start using physical associations and stories to remember names, you'll be amazed at how they stick."

Robert promised to give the technique a try. His meditation session earlier in the day and its immediate positive effect had reminded him how important it was to try new ways of doing things.

"Thanks a lot for the nice things that you've said about me when introducing me to others," Robert said.

Albert reassured him that he meant every word of praise. He said he tried to elevate other people as much as possible when introducing them to others.

"I've noticed something else tonight," Robert said. "Some people jump quickly from one conversation to another, as if they are trying to meet as many people as possible. You take your time and seem to enjoy drawing people into long conversations."

Albert smiled. "Too many people think of networking as a numbers game. They believe that the more people they meet, the more success they'll have. Actually, the opposite is true. When people dwell on the size of their network instead of the quality of their connections, they tend to alienate others, because they make them feel like targets.

"My father always told me that we have two ears and one mouth and that we should use them in proportion. By asking good questions and listening carefully, I learn a lot. For instance, I always try to figure out what a person wants to achieve. When I focus on helping people reach their goals, it's a sure thing that many will want to do business with me and will send their friends my way."

Albert glanced across the room and appeared to spot a familiar face. "Okay, time to step down from my soapbox," he said. "Let's go over there so I can introduce you to Anthony Sanderson. He runs a local sailing school and is not only a great friend but also one of the best networkers I know."

Like all of Albert's friends, Anthony was enthusiastic about meeting Robert. However, he didn't have much time to speak because he needed to get home to put his daughter to bed. Before leaving, he invited Robert to drop by his sailing club the following night for one of his monthly salons. Robert had no idea what a salon was, but his curiosity was piqued. He agreed to attend.

"Be sure to get there early—half an hour, at least," Anthony cautioned him. "It's a popular event."

14

A Gathering Place

DRIVING INTO THE PARKING lot of the two-story sailing school, Robert noticed a line of about fifty people waiting to get into the building. He rolled down his car window and asked an elegant sixty-something man with a bow tie and a toothy smile whether he was in the right place for the salon.

The man exclaimed, "You certainly are, and you're in for a treat! I've been coming to these events for the past five years, and I've only missed one. Grab a parking space before they fill up, and I'll introduce you around."

Robert parked his car and chatted with Paul Simmons, the man who had greeted him so warmly. Thirty minutes later, Anthony came out to address the crowd.

"Good evening!" Anthony stood on a stool in front of the main entrance and spoke into a mike. "It's wonderful to see so many familiar faces and friends-to-be. I want to get as many of you inside as possible, but I can't afford to anger the fire marshal. There's going to be a live simulcast of the event on a big screen in the tent across the parking lot. You'll find plenty of food and drinks in the tent, so please don't be upset if I direct you there."

Anthony opened the doors and the crowd moved forward patiently. When Robert reached the entrance, Anthony gave him a hug as if he'd known him forever. "Wonderful to see you again! I'm glad you met Paul. He's a great guy and one of the first members of the club. I hope you can stick around a bit after the presentation so I can introduce you to more people."

Robert followed the crowd into a large wood-paneled room full of nautical knickknacks and sailboat photos and paintings. White director's chairs with blue canvas seat covers were lined up in rows facing a podium and a large screen.

"Come sit here." Paul patted the chair next to him, and Robert did as instructed.

"Robert, this is Brian," Paul said, introducing a tall, sandy-haired man in his mid-fifties sitting on his other side. "He's been a member of the club for thirty years, about as long as I have. He's a sea dog, too. You can't find a better crew member than Brian."

Just then, Anthony walked to the podium. "Welcome! For those who of you who have been to previous salons, thanks for coming. For first-timers, it's great to see you. We've been doing salons like tonight's event at the club about ten times a year for the past five years. We always try to bring in speakers who have interesting ideas worth sharing as a way to educate and inspire meaningful conversations and a sense of community amongst our members and their guests.

"It's my pleasure to introduce tonight's speaker, Barbara Cordon. Barbara is president of the Sustainability Institute, one of the largest environmental education non-profit organizations in the country. As is the custom at our salons, Barbara will speak for forty-five minutes, and then we'll have fifteen minutes for Q&A. After that, I hope you'll be able join us in the tent in the parking lot to see old friends, make new ones, and discuss ideas."

Barbara delivered a dynamic presentation with sobering examples of environmental challenges facing the world and innovative ways that people working together could make a positive difference.

Robert listened with interest so he could share what he was learning with Marion and Andrea, as they both were avid environmentalists. He also reflected on the business benefits of sponsoring salons that attracted some of the most important movers and shakers in the community. Clearly, the high attendance indicated that Anthony was providing his sailing club members with something they valued—which made it likely that they would continue paying their membership dues. At the same time, he was increasing awareness of his sailing school in the community, since the event was open to all.

After the lively Q&A session, the crowd converged under the tent for a post-event mixer. Animated conversations were taking place everywhere. Robert bought beer for himself, Paul, and Brian. He shared with them how his wife and daughter were constantly reminding him to recycle and that the speaker had provided so many compelling reasons to live in the environmentally conscious way that they encouraged.

Then, glancing at his watch, Robert said, "Gentlemen, I have a busy day planned for tomorrow, so I have to go home now. It has been a real pleasure meeting you, and I hope to see you at the next salon. Before leaving, I wanted to thank Anthony for inviting me. Have you seen him?"

"Wait just a second," Brian said. "We didn't get a chance to find out what it is that you do for a living."

Robert explained that he owned an insurance agency founded by his great-grandfather. "See," Paul told Brian, "there *are* things in this town older than me!"

Brian laughed and turned back to Robert. "Your timing is good," he said. "Insurance rates for my restaurant group have skyrocketed. I'd love to get some ideas on how we might save money on insurance. Give me a call next week and we'll set up a time to talk." With that, Brian handed Robert his card.

It was one of Robert's best leads that month. Albert's wisdom about networking was indeed true. Success comes from taking a genuine interest in others—and not worrying about turning every conversation into a business opportunity.

15

Connecting Online

ROBERT ARRIVED AT THE office early the following morning. He loved being the first person at work; it gave him an opportunity to plan his day when things were still quiet. It also allowed him to prioritize the many new ideas bouncing around in his head.

"Hey, Dad!" Andrea leaned her head into his office. "Why didn't you give me a ride this morning?"

Robert looked up in surprise. Andrea was usually one of the last to arrive at the office. "Sorry, honey; I thought that you would be coming in later."

"I wanted to get an early start with my online networking. You know, before all the distractions."

Robert smiled. *She and I are alike in so many ways.* There was one big difference, though. Andrea and the other young employees were spending work hours on social media to build connections—and they were getting positive results.

"I don't really understand the whole online networking thing," Robert admitted. "You'll have to explain it to me sometime."

"How about now? We've got time." She pulled up a chair next to his.

"Uh, sure," Robert said. He believed that online networking could be a great way to develop business—even if he didn't fully understand it. He had committed to trying new things; well, now was as good a time as any to give online networking a try.

Andrea suggested that he find out how to do more with LinkedIn. With two fingers, Robert slowly pecked his user name and password into the website.

"Why do you have only ninety-seven connections on LinkedIn, Dad?" Andrea asked as she looked at the computer screen. "You know more people than anyone I know."

Robert confessed that he rarely used LinkedIn because he didn't really understand it. He told Andrea that he sometimes accepted people's connection requests, but he never asked others to connect with him.

Robert brightened when a screen popped up on LinkedIn recommending forty-seven people to connect with. "Hey look! I can invite these people into my online network with just one click. This technology is amazing."

Andrea warned him, "Don't take the bait, Dad. If you click on that button, all those people will just get a generic email message from you inviting them to become one of your LinkedIn connections."

Robert certainly didn't want to do that. "I can't stand those generic invitations," he said. "They're just like junk mail that we get addressed to 'Dear Occupant.'"

"Exactly. Whether you're networking in the real

world or online, you have to keep things personal. When you send a connection request or respond to one, you should write as if you are addressing a friend."

With that in mind, Robert found Anthony Sanderson's LinkedIn profile and sent him this connection request:

I had a wonderful time yesterday. You've inspired me to host a similar series of events at my agency in the coming year, and I'd be honored to have you as our first speaker. I'll be in touch soon to set things up. In the meantime, it would be great to stay connected on LinkedIn.

Andrea read Robert's message. "Now that's what I'm talking about! When you send a message like that on LinkedIn, you're building the foundation of a solid relationship both online *and* offline."

Andrea asked him to think about businesspeople he admired and whether anyone stood out as exceptional. Robert remembered driving through his neighborhood that morning and seeing a "For Sale" sign with Kate Charles listed as the realtor. It seemed as if half the real estate signs he saw these days in the neighborhood belonged to Kate. This didn't surprise him, given Kate's knowledge, friendliness, and business savvy.

Robert asked, "How about Kate Charles?'"

"Perfect!" Andrea suggested that Robert type Kate's name into the LinkedIn search box to see whether she was one of his professional connections. To Robert's surprise, he was already connected to her. Clearly, this was a testament to her networking savvy, since all his current connections were people who had reached out to him first.

"Since you're connected to Kate, you can write an online recommendation for her," Andrea said. "It needs to be only a few sentences or a short paragraph. It's important that you make it heartfelt and specific. Focus on a few things that make Kate a great realtor, based on the experiences you've had with her."

There were many positive things Robert could write about Kate. So, after gathering his thoughts, he wrote this recommendation:

In the 15 years I've known Kate, she has impressed me with her professionalism and people skills. A few years ago, I recommended her to my mother, who interviewed five different realtors before choosing Kate to sell her home. It was a wise decision. Kate suggested minor improvements like painting the kitchen and updating the master bathroom. We did everything she recommended, and the house sold for well above the list price in less than a week. If I were going to sell my home, I would choose Kate as my realtor, and I feel confident recommending her.

"Nicely done," Andrea said. "Now just click 'Send.' See how easy that was?"

Robert was relieved. LinkedIn wasn't nearly as complicated as he thought. Andrea explained that she scheduled just thirty minutes a week to work on LinkedIn, from sending out personal connection requests to responding to invitations, writing recommendations, and searching for people in her network she could connect to each other. That seemed even more manageable.

Just then, Robert's smartphone rang. "Kate Charles" appeared on the display.

"Robert, how are you?" A smile was audible in Kate's voice. "Your LinkedIn recommendation was such a terrific way to start the day. Thank you so much."

Robert's recommendation was particularly meaningful, she explained, because she hadn't asked him to write it—indeed, it was only the second unsolicited LinkedIn recommendation she had received.

"I would love to have lunch with you next week," said Kate. "My treat, of course!"

16

Changing Times

IT HAD BEEN ONLY six months since Robert met Albert, but he already felt that an enormous black cloud had lifted. The spreadsheets he used to track the agency's performance provided clear indicators as to why he felt better. Compared to the same six months in the previous year, policy renewals were up 15 percent, and new policies had jumped by the same amount. Referrals from current clients to prospective insurance buyers had increased by more than a third. Also, four months had passed without his needing a credit card cash advance to cover payroll. He no longer stayed up late at night worried about being able to pay his employees and his mortgage.

Robert was convinced that his openness to new ways of building business relationships had galvanized his employees to do the same. However, some were still struggling. For instance, Peter Constanza, one of his longest-tenured agents, saw a continued decline in policy renewals and referrals. This was in keeping with a five-year downward trend in which Peter underperformed his peers.

Robert had avoided a confrontation with Peter

because he hoped that the renewed energy of his coworkers would inspire him to adopt a better approach to work. Yet as time passed with no improvements, Robert knew that he had to do something. He texted Peter: *"Please come to my office ASAP. We need to talk."*

The buzz of his smartphone interrupted Peter's conversation with Sam. "It's probably just my wife telling me what to pick up on the way home," he laughed. When he glanced at his phone and saw Robert's message, he felt his pulse quicken. "Sam, I've got to run."

Walking to Robert's office, Peter reflected on how he had lost his passion for being an insurance agent. When he started with the agency twenty-three years ago, he'd enjoyed the challenge of building a book of clients and even looked forward to coming in to work early to make cold calls. Now, with an ever-shrinking client base, the need to rebuild his business made him feel exhausted.

"Have a seat." Robert gestured toward his visitor's chair. "I was reviewing our quarterly numbers and noticed some good news and bad news. On the positive side, the agency just completed its best quarter in years. On the down side, you continue to struggle. What's going on?"

Robert had anticipated a defensive response. Instead, Peter sighed. "Honestly, my heart just isn't in the job anymore. You're encouraging us to build relationships with existing clients and find new ones, but I simply don't have the energy."

"So what's keeping you here?" Robert asked.

"Retirement! I'm eight years away from collecting Social Security, and I need to keep building my 401(k) before I quit."

"Eight years is too long to do a job that you don't enjoy. If you could be doing something other than working here, what would it be?"

Peter didn't hesitate. "Well, now that my kids are away at college, I realize how much I miss being around young people. If I could make it work financially, I would teach junior or senior high school students."

"Well, why don't you just go for it? Our schools certainly need committed teachers," Robert said. "What if we work out a plan to transition your clients to other agents over a few years while you work here part-time? That way, you would have time to go to school and get your teaching certificate while still generating income."

Peter was flabbergasted. He couldn't understand why Robert didn't just fire him. And he said as much.

"You've contributed a lot to this agency over the years," Robert said. "I'm very grateful for that. Helping you pursue your passion is the right thing to do."

Peter still couldn't quite believe what he was hearing. He thanked Robert profusely before bounding out of his boss's office.

Later that afternoon, Robert called Andrea at her desk. "We should leave now to make it to 'Family Dinner' at the retirement home on time. Meet me at the elevator in five minutes."

In the elevator, Andrea said, "Everyone was buzzing about your conversation with Peter today. After you two spoke, he walked around the office with a big smile on his face, announcing that he was going back to school to get a teaching certificate. I've never seen him so happy. It's cool that you're encouraging him to make this career transition. But I am somewhat surprised."

"Helping Peter move on to something that inspires him is the right thing to do. He's been a loyal employee, so he deserves our support. The agency benefits, too. His long-term clients won't feel like they're being abandoned, because Peter will help transition them to their new agents.

"To grow the agency, we can't just keep on doing what we've always done. Everybody needs to be creative and willing to build relationships that fuel our growth. Encouraging Peter to pursue his passion for teaching makes sense for him—and for us."

17

Wedding Bells

"FAMILY DINNER" WAS A monthly event that the Hansons had looked forward to ever since Hillhaven hired a classically trained French chef whose dishes rivaled anything served in the town's finest restaurants.

Marion was already waiting on their front steps. "Guess what?" she said. "I had a chat with Joan this afternoon. Apparently she has some big news to share with us tonight."

Robert wondered aloud whether anything could be wrong. "I doubt it," Marion exclaimed. "Your mother was positively giddy!"

Andrea chuckled. "I hear wedding bells."

At Hillhaven, they parked next to Albert, who had arrived at the same time. Together, they walked to the main lobby.

The big dining hall was decorated with red and white streamers. Around two hundred residents sat at round tables of eight set with porcelain plates and elegant silverware, and a vase of beautiful red roses.

Hillhaven Executive Director Shirley Johnson stepped up to the podium to welcome the residents and guests. Once everyone had taken their seats, the "Wedding March" began to play over the room's loud-speakers and a hushed silence fell over the audience. Fred entered the dining hall first, with Joan pushing his freshly polished wheelchair. He looked elegant in a black tuxedo. Joan wore a flowing purple dress with purple and white flowers in her hair. The room erupted in loud applause. Both were smiling ear-to-ear as they made their way to the front of the room.

A Hillhaven employee held a microphone for Fred. "Well folks, today I can confirm that I'm officially the luckiest man alive. I decided that I was going to ask for Joan's hand in marriage on the night of my one hundredth birthday. But, it took me until last week to get my courage up to ask. Would you believe that she said 'Yes'?"

Joan laughed and grabbed the microphone. "Oh Fred! If somebody had told me a few years ago that I would marry again, I wouldn't have believed them. But, of course, I didn't know *you* then. To set the record straight, I didn't hesitate for a second when you popped the question."

"Well, thank goodness," Fred replied. "I'm not getting any younger, you know."

After the audience cheered loudly, Joan shared that she and Fred had decided not to waste any time and had secretly married in a civil ceremony at City Hall just a couple of days ago.

She concluded, "This evening is all about celebrating our marriage with family and friends."

The Hansons and Albert jumped up from the table to hug the bride and groom. Albert raised his champagne glass. "A toast to a beautiful bride and dapper groom. May they live a happy and fulfilling life together." Turning to Robert, Marion, and Andrea, he continued: "I couldn't be more thrilled that our families are now bound together through such a wonderful union."

As waiters made their way around the dining room to pour champagne and serve slices of wedding cake, Robert walked over to Fred and knelt down next to his wheelchair. "Sir, I just want to tell you how grateful I am for the tremendous joy you've brought my mother."

"It's your mother who has given me more happiness than I could have ever expected at this stage in my life. Also, for goodness sake, please stop calling me sir. It's Fred now that we're family!"

"Fred it is," Robert said. "How can I help you and Mom get settled into your new life?"

"Well, it would be great if you could come by tomorrow morning to help move my belongings into her apartment," Fred replied. "Now that we're officially married, it's time I officially moved in with her, too."

"It would be my honor, sir," Robert said. "Oops! I mean Fred."

18

Passing the Torch

ROBERT GOT UP EARLY the next morning and slipped out of bed without waking Marion. He padded downstairs to the kitchen and loaded the blender with a healthy mix of fruit, greens, coconut milk, and ice.

The roads were empty as Robert drove to Hillhaven. He was looking forward to speaking with Fred alone, as his father-in-law's usual entourage of friends was likely still asleep.

Robert knocked softly on the door of Fred's small single apartment. "Come in," Fred said heartily. He was sitting in his wheelchair at a small kitchen table drinking a smoothie that rivaled Robert's not only in its size but also in its bright green color.

Robert grinned. "Great minds think alike," he said. "I've been having those for breakfast myself."

"I bet Albert had something to do with that. I always did tell him that a natural diet loaded with fruits and vegetables is the only way to go. Lots of physical exercise, too. Speaking of which, shall we get started?"

Under Fred's watchful gaze, Robert started carefully packing up the centenarian's belongings in the small office adjoining the kitchen. An old-fashioned roll-top desk dominated the room. On the walls were yellowed diplomas and old family photographs, including pictures of Fred in his World War II infantryman uniform.

Centered on one of the walls was a gold-framed photo of a dapper gentleman with a handlebar mustache. Robert did a double take and leaned closer to examine the image.

Fred was smiling. "I guessed that you would spot your great-grandfather Benjamin Hanson. He was a great man."

Robert was dumbfounded. "I recognized him because we had the same photo in our dining room when I was kid. I wish I knew more about him. Since he died when I was just three or four, all I know about Great-grandfather Benjamin is what my parents told me. Did you know him well?"

"I sure did. When I returned from World War II, I went to work for a large brokerage house. Some of my first cold calls were to the Hanson Insurance Agency. I remember trying to meet with Benjamin Hanson three times, but his secretary wouldn't let me near him. She sure was one tough gatekeeper." Fred chuckled at the memory. "On my fourth visit, your great-grandfather saw me through his office window and waved me into his office, much to his secretary's consternation."

Fred explained that he had been excited to meet one of the town's most well-respected business leaders. At that first meeting, not wanting to waste an opportunity, Fred launched into a well-rehearsed sales pitch.

Listening politely, the elder Hanson had waited about twenty seconds until Fred stopped to take a breath. "Son," he had interrupted, "wait just a minute. I know your family, and I know that you came back from fighting in France. We'll have plenty of time to talk about business, but right now I want to hear all about your service in Europe."

Recalling that day now, Fred beamed. "I spent a good hour talking with him about my military service, and he shared his World War I army experiences with me. That was the beginning of a friendship and a business relationship that lasted until his death. For nearly twenty-five years, he mentored me in every aspect of business."

Robert didn't know what to say. He vaguely remembered hearing family stories about Benjamin Hanson's business acumen, but he had never heard any specifics. "What do you remember most about him?" he asked Fred.

"Well, he was naturally gifted at sales. He taught me that building relationships is the key to selling. Over those twenty-five years, he introduced me to many brilliant business people who were also great connectors. Without his guidance and what I learned from his friends, my company would never have become the success that it is today.

"There's one more thing you should know: he would be incredibly proud to see what you're doing now with the agency he founded."

Robert was puzzled. "What do you mean?"

"I understand that Albert has been mentoring you over the past six months and introducing you to business people we both admire. By connecting you with great relationship builders, Albert is helping me make good on a pledge that I made to your great-grandfather. I promised him that I would pass along what I learned from his mentoring."

Robert reflected on this information as he carefully removed his great-grandfather's photograph from the wall and carefully wrapped it and added it to a box. Lost in his thoughts, he didn't hear Albert come in. But when he turned, Albert was standing beside him.

"You look mesmerized," Albert said.

"Well, it does feel that way. Your father was just telling me about my great-grandfather!"

Albert responded, "He was amazing. Without his guidance, we never would have accomplished as much in business as we have."

"How come you didn't seek me out years ago when I could have really used his wisdom?"

"That's a fair question," replied Albert. "If Fred and I had known that you were struggling, of course we would have shared everything that your great-grandfather taught us. But, we assumed your agency was doing fine. We should have checked in with you sooner."

"It's not your fault," Robert said. "I should have realized years ago that I needed help to turn the agency around—but I was too proud to reach out and ask for it."

"Here, Robert, take this." Fred handed him an old brass key. "In that desk drawer, you'll find the most valuable lessons that I learned from your great-grandfather. I wrote them down nearly seventy years ago, and they are just as important today as they were then. One of my life's greatest joys has been sharing these principles with people who need them.

"Some folks I've shared the list with have told me that the principles are too simplistic. They mistakenly believe that complex strategies and tactics are necessary for business success. But time and time again I've seen how your great-grandfather's simple wisdom is all people need to succeed."

Looking at his father, Albert said, "You're absolutely right." Then he turned to Robert. "Our mentoring days are winding to a close, and we want to make sure that your ancestor's wisdom outlives us."

Robert unlocked the desk drawer with excitement and removed a brittle piece of yellowed paper with a list written in Fred's elegant cursive handwriting. He read it quickly and knew exactly what he would do.

19

Celebration

ROBERT AND MARION STOOD outside their favorite Italian restaurant and welcomed employees to the first Christmas party outside the office in over ten years. With Hanson Insurance Agency growing and the future looking bright for the first time in years, it was time to celebrate.

Albert, Joan, and Fred pulled up in Albert's convertible. While Albert helped his father out of the car and into his wheelchair, Joan joined Robert and Marion.

"How's my favorite newlywed?" Robert asked. Joan beamed and gave her son and daughter-in-law big hugs; then they maneuvered Fred's wheelchair over the curb and into the restaurant.

Robert guided his family to their seats at a round table at the front of the banquet room. The attendees included agency employees and their family members as well as longtime friends. Many of the people Albert had introduced to Robert over the past six months and whose ideas had helped bring new life to the agency were also there.

Standing at a podium, Robert welcomed the guests. "Our family is thrilled that you've come to celebrate the hard work and creativity of the entire Hanson Insurance Agency team as we're wrapping up our best year in over a decade.

"I want to give special thanks to Fred, and his son, Albert, who showed me through their words and actions how to build a successful business. Also, I'm grateful for the many people Albert introduced me to, who taught me what it takes to create strong relationships that result in client loyalty and referrals."

Andrea was standing by and brought a microphone to Fred, who cleared his throat and began to speak.

"When I met Robert six months ago, I was reminded of the struggles that I faced more than seventy years ago when my business career began. Fortunately, one of my first sales calls was to your agency's founder and Robert's great-grandfather, Benjamin Hanson. He took me under his wing and taught me how to build personal and professional connections that were the foundation of my success. Albert and I have enjoyed sharing with Robert what Benjamin Hanson taught us. And we admire how Robert has communicated the lessons he has learned with all of you and how you have implemented them so successfully."

Loud applause rang out.

"Thanks, Fred," Robert said. "We absolutely wouldn't be celebrating here tonight without the tremendous insights you and Albert provided."

He gazed around the room. "I hope you enjoy the evening. Before you leave, I invite you to pick up a framed version of the principles that Fred set down seventy years ago, based on what he learned from our founder. I ask only that you commit to sharing this wisdom to help others. In so doing, you will honor my mentors and our founder. Now, without further ado, enjoy the festivities!"

Fred and Albert beamed, knowing that Benjamin Hanson's wisdom would continue making a difference.

20

Continuing the Legacy

THE NEXT DAY, ANDREA had just finished hanging her gold-framed copy of her great-great-grandfather's wisdom on her cubicle wall when May called from the front desk. Sally Elkins had arrived for a nine o'clock appointment.

"Thanks, May. Please send her back."

Sally was a young realtor Andrea had met at a chamber of commerce mixer a few weeks earlier. When they spoke then, Andrea had sensed that something was weighing on Sally's mind. She had invited her to come by the office to see how she might be able to help.

Now she greeted her warmly and suggested they go down to the lobby coffee shop to talk.

"That sounds great," said Sally. "I could sure use another dose of caffeine to lift me up. Things just haven't been clicking for me like I thought they would when I opened my own real estate agency last year."

"I know the feeling," Andrea said. "Not too long ago, everyone here was feeling pretty down about our business. Then amazing things started to happen!"

Pointing to the framed words on the wall behind

her desk, Andrea added: "And it's all because of those ideas."

Intrigued, Sally walked up for a closer look.

Seven Rules
for Building Business
One Relationship at a Time

ONE — Nurture body and mind to create positive energy and enthusiasm that attracts others.

TWO — Seek out individuals who expose you to new ways of thinking.

THREE — Ask your connections how you can be of service to them.

FOUR — Serve others without consideration for how you will benefit.

FIVE — Exceed expectations.

SIX — Let people know how they can help you succeed.

SEVEN — Be grateful.

Acknowledgments

THIS BOOK WOULD NEVER have happened without the inspiring lessons I've learned from many great connectors including Anthony Sandberg, Mike Faith, Paul Witkay, Noah Oken-Berg, Jim Perucca, Bob Horn, Steve Stogner, Shari Storm, Bob Canter, Bob Rosson, Jeff Capen, João Moura, André Moura, Mark Herdering, Jordan Adler, Kody Bateman, Kellie Poulsen-Grill, Kristi Govertsen, Mike Sandoval, Agustin Enriquez, Scott Burns, Dev Dion, and Seth Weinstein.

I am fortunate to have old friends who have always shared their wisdom and encouraged me to pursue my dreams. Marty Duffy, Wade Freeman, Nathan Blain, Pere Prat, Eric Rothberg, Alex Gorodisher, and Mark Ungar, just writing your names brings a smile to my face.

Allison Clarke, Bill Conerly, Jathan Janove, and Cathey Armillas, your advice and counsel have shaped this book and my speaking career in positive ways that you cannot even imagine.

I'm grateful for the advice that I received from my friends and talented authors Richard Fenton and

Andrea Waltz who helped me bring the characters in the book to life. You inspire me to aim higher and dig deeper.

Kristi Hein, Dick Margulis, and Ranilo Cabo, thank you for your editing and design skills. The quality of your work is evident throughout these pages.

Mom, Dad, Martha, Jeff, Chris, Renate, and Guenther, your love and support have made me a better person.

Finally, words cannot express how lucky I am to have such a wonderful wife and daughter. Ellen, your eagle-eye, love, and encouragement galvanized me to finish this book. Anya, a great connector in your own right, I appreciate your allowing me to write when you really just wanted me to play with you. I love both of you more than the sun, the moon, and the stars. And I always will.

About the Author

PATRICK GALVIN COFOUNDED The Galvanizing Group, a brand strategy consulting and marketing firm in Portland, Oregon, in 2002. As the firm's "chief galvanizer," he has galvanized the growth of hundreds of businesses, from sole proprietorships to publicly traded companies, by helping clients create the connections that increase loyalty, referrals, and sales.

Patrick earned an MBA in international marketing from Thunderbird, one of the world's top-ranked international business programs. Upon graduation, he worked as the international sales manager for an industrial and agricultural equipment manufacturer and built a profitable sales network throughout Canada and South America where none had existed. He subsequently became president of his family's furniture stores. Under his leadership, sales rose 300% in three years.

Patrick graduated *cum laude* from Georgetown University with a BS in foreign service. He received a Rotary International Scholarship for postgraduate studies at the University of São Paulo, Brazil. He is an enthusiastic member of the Rotary Club of Portland, where he has served in various leadership positions, and he is a past president of the Oregon Chapter of the National Speakers Association.

A dog lover, Patrick cowrote *Secrets of a Working Dog: Unleash Your Potential and Create Success*, which illustrates how humans can work smarter and be happier, from the perspective of his wise and witty boxer dog, Bella. *Publisher's Weekly* called the book "delightful and insightful."

Patrick and his wife, Ellen, and daughter, Anya, live in Portland, Oregon, where they enjoy a variety of outdoor activities. In addition to his native English, Patrick is fluent in Spanish and Portuguese. You can reach him at patrick@galvanizinggroup.com.

Bring *The Connector's Way* to Your Company, Conference or Event

THE CONNECTOR'S WAY is the creation of author and professional speaker Patrick Galvin. Patrick helps teams and organizations develop the strategies and techniques that build strong connections and galvanize success.

Patrick takes great pride in delivering high-quality keynote presentations, breakout sessions, and workshops that engage audiences with fresh and practical material. He tailors his message to meet the unique needs of every audience. After hundreds of appearances, he has never given the same speech twice. As a result, he has received enthusiastic testimonials from organizations and associations in a variety of industries throughout the United States, Canada, Latin America, and Europe.

For information on having Patrick work with your organization or to book Patrick for your next meeting or event, visit www.PatrickGalvin.com or call 503-249-8800.

Ordering multiple books for your company, team or group event? Volume discounts are available by contacting info@galvanizinggroup.com.